T0063732

Let's get gardening

DK

DK | Penguin Random House

Senior editor **Satu Hämeenaho-Fox**
Designer **Rachael Hare**
Design assistants **Eleanor Bates, Kitty Glavin**
Art editors **Seepiya Sahni, Jaileen Kaur**
Senior art editor **Nidhi Mehra**
Editor **Radhika Haswani**
US Senior editor **Shannon Beatty**
Americanizer **Margaret Parrish**
Picture researcher **Sakshi Saluja**
Pre-production producer **Dragana Puvacic**
Producer **John Casey**
Jacket designer **Rachael Hare**
Jacket co-ordinator **Isobel Walsh**
Managing editor **Penny Smith**
Managing art editor **Mabel Chan**
Creative director **Helen Senior**
Publishing director **Sarah Larter**

Published in the United States by DK Publishing
1450 Broadway, Suite 801, New York, NY 10018

Copyright © 2019 DK, a Division of
Penguin Random House LLC
21 22 23 10 9 8 7 6 5 4
012–314398–Feb/2020

All rights reserved.
Without limiting the rights under the copyright
reserved above, no part of this publication may
be reproduced, stored in or introduced into a
retrieval system, or transmitted, in any form,
or by any means (electronic, mechanical,
photocopying, recording, or otherwise),
without the prior written permission
of the copyright owner.

Published in Great Britain by Dorling Kindersley
Limited. A catalog record for this book is
available from the Library of Congress.
ISBN: 978-1-4654-8549-6

DK books are available at special discounts
when purchased in bulk for sales promotions,
premiums, fund-raising, or educational use. For
details, contact: DK Publishing Special Markets,
1450 Broadway, 8th Floor, New York, NY 10018
SpecialSales@dk.com

Printed and bound in China

A WORLD OF IDEAS:
SEE ALL THERE IS TO KNOW

www.dk.com

This book contains content previously
published in DK titles *How Does My
Garden Grow?*; *Ready, Set, Grow!*;
Grow It, Cook It; and *Wildlife Gardening*.

Contents

4 Be an eco-friendly gardener
6 What is a plant?
8 What plants need
10 Gardening tools

12 Kitchen garden
14 What is a kitchen garden?
16 Growing herbs
18 How to grow carrots
20 How to grow potatoes
22 How to grow beets
24 How to grow lettuce
26 How to grow leeks
28 How to grow spinach
30 How to grow chilies
32 How to grow eggplant
34 How to grow zucchini
36 How to grow pumpkins
38 How to grow beans
40 How to grow peppers
42 How to grow corn
44 How to grow tomatoes
46 How to grow blueberries
48 How to grow strawberries
50 How to grow lemons

52 Wildlife garden
54 Why be a wildlife gardener?
56 Your garden is a habitat
58 Your seasonal wildlife garden
60 A wildlife hedge
62 Plants for a fragrant garden
64 Starting plants for wildlife
66 Sunflowers

68 Mini nature preserve
70 Plant a tree
72 Water plants
74 Pond life
76 Pond dipping
78 Container pond
80 Make a frog and toad home
82 Plants for bees
84 Create a bee hotel
86 Ladybug sanctuary
88 Plants for caterpillars
   and butterflies
90 Butterfly feeder
92 Pets' corner

94 Recycling garden
96 Why recycle in the garden?
98 Recycle and renew
100 Collecting seeds
102 Eggshell planters
104 Stunning succulents
106 Cork planters
108 Creative containers
110 Pot labels and markers
112 Mini greenhouses
114 Strawberry boots
116 Bird bathroom
118 Bird feeder
120 Owl nesting boot
122 Self-watering seedlings
124 Glossary
126 Index
128 Acknowledgments

Be an eco-friendly gardener

Being eco-friendly means thinking about how what we do affects nature, from tiny seedlings to huge trees, and the animals that rely on them. It's also about keeping in mind that you are part of nature, too. Get out there and get gardening!

What does an eco-friendly gardener do?

Grows vegetables

Vegetables that you grow yourself are by far the best. They are tasty and healthy to eat, save money, and help the environment by reducing pollution from the vehicles that carry them to supermarkets. No plastic packaging here!

Protects wildlife

We can attract wildlife to our gardens by planting plants that encourage animals to visit, and by giving them a safe home. Gardens are vital habitats for animals in cities, where many areas have been paved over.

Reduces waste

We can reuse and recycle things from the home so we don't have to throw them away. Food waste can be used as compost, while broken items can find a new purpose in the garden.

Makes home greener

Bring plants inside to help make your home prettier and healthier. Plants clean the air and make for a much nicer indoor environment.

Gets healthy

Gardening is good for you! Research has shown that digging in the soil makes you feel happier, and it's also good exercise.

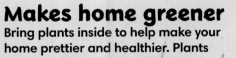

What is a plant?

A plant is a living thing that makes food from sunlight. There are nearly 400,000 types of plant! They have flowers, leaves, stems, and roots.

Flowers
Many plants create new life using flowers. Once the flowers have been fertilized, they produce seeds or fruit.

Leaves
A plant's leaves capture energy from sunlight to turn into food. Tiny openings let gases and moisture in and out of the plant.

Stem
Stems act as a transportation network to take water, minerals, and food to all parts of the plant. They also produce leaves and new shoots along their length.

Fruit

Root hairs
These absorb water from the soil.

Roots
Roots suck up the water and nutrients from the soil that the plant needs to grow.

Root tip
This part grows into the soil.

How do plants grow?

Seed leaf

True leaf

Seeds contain everything a new plant needs to grow: the baby plant itself and the food to get it started.

When the conditions are right, the seed takes in water, swells, and splits its case. The main root reaches down into the soil.

One or two tiny seed leaves shoot out, quickly followed by the first true leaves. The seedling can now make its own food.

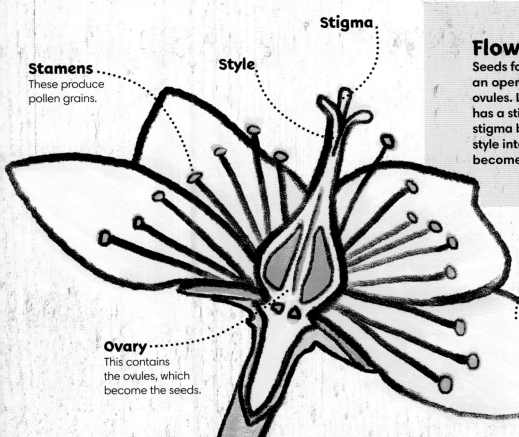

Stigma

Style

Stamens
These produce pollen grains.

Ovary
This contains the ovules, which become the seeds.

Petals
Bright colors attract insects.

Flowers: the inside story

Seeds form inside flowers. At the base of a flower there is an open part called the ovary, which contains eggs, called ovules. Leading to the ovary is a tube called the style, which has a sticky end called a stigma. Pollen is carried onto the stigma by the wind or insects. The pollen travels down the style into the ovary and combines with the ovules to become seeds.

Bees
and other insects help pollinate flowers.

What Plants need

Plants adapt to their environments—some like hot, dry weather, some like lots of rain, while others prefer sandy soil. Whenever you buy a plant from a garden center, or grow one from seed, make sure you give it what it needs to thrive.

Check the labels

Read labels and seed packets when you buy plants and seeds. These tell you:
- What the plant will look like
- When to sow
- How to sow
- When to plant out in the yard
- When to harvest
- If the plant likes sun or shade
- The type of soil it prefers

These tomatoes have grape-size fruit in bunches—ideal for hanging baskets.

☐ Sow	● Plant out	○ Harvest	
Spring	Summer	Fall	Winter

Sowing and growing

- Sow indoors in early spring
- Sow seeds ¼ in (6 mm) deep in free-draining seed compost
- Plant outdoors in late spring or early summer
- Harvest late summer to fall
- Likes full sun
- Prefers warm, well-drained soil

The front of the seed packet shows the variety of the plant and what it will look like when fully grown.

Soil

This is vital to plants. It anchors their roots and acts as a store of water and nutrients. Not all soils are the same, so gardeners often add compost made from dead plant material (like you'd find on a compost heap) to their soil to improve it.

Seed compost

A fine-textured mix that holds water well. It is low in nutrients because seeds already have their own supply of food.

All-purpose compost

An all-around compost mixture that looks like soil. Most plants in this book will grow well in all-purpose compost.

Grow-bag compost

This is a nutrient-rich mixture specially prepared for hungry vegetables, such as peppers.

Sunlight

Like people, plants need energy to grow and reproduce. But unlike people, plants make their own food through a process called photosynthesis. To do this, plants take in carbon dioxide gas (CO_2) from the air and water from the soil, then use sunlight to convert them into glucose (a type of sugar). The plants then release waste oxygen gas (O_2) into the air.

Carbon dioxide +
water + sunlight
= glucose + oxygen

O_2

CO_2

Water

Water

Without water, plants wilt and die. However, most plants don't like waterlogged roots, so make holes in the bottom of the container and add broken pot pieces or small stones to help the water drain. Always water plants before and after you plant them in a new pot.

Broken pot

Peat-based compost

Carnivorous (meat-eating) plants, such as sundews, need peat-based compost. Sometimes coir (coconut) fiber is used instead of peat.

Aquatic soil

This contains a slow-release fertilizer that does not leak into water, preventing algae and weeds from growing in the pond. Ordinary garden soil can also be used.

Mulch

Mulches cover soil and help keep it moist. They also stop weeds from growing. Typical mulches include small stones, shells, straw, and wood chips.

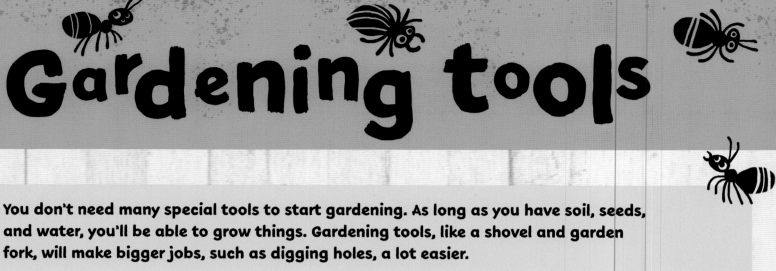

Gardening tools

You don't need many special tools to start gardening. As long as you have soil, seeds, and water, you'll be able to grow things. Gardening tools, like a shovel and garden fork, will make bigger jobs, such as digging holes, a lot easier.

For gardening outdoors

Garden fork
For breaking up the soil so plants can spread their roots.

Shovel
For digging holes in the soil.

Trowel
For filling pots and covering seeds with soil.

Plant pots
Collect pots of varying sizes for different plants.

Watering can
For watering indoor and outdoor plants.

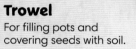

Gardening gloves
Thick gloves for dealing with rough or prickly plants.

Access to water
All plants need water to grow.

Liquid plant food
Food for plants that need extra nutrients.

Compost
Rich compost gives plants a better chance to grow than ordinary soil.

For gardening indoors

Plastic bottle
Useful for various gardening projects.

Spray bottle
For spritzing delicate plants, such as ferns.

Pot and tray
Helps keep your plants moist on the windowsill.

Glass jar
For storage and craft projects.

Soil
For planting your seeds and plants in.

Gravel
Makes your plant projects look neater and deters slugs.

Tools for making things

Colored pencils
For decorating labels and creating papercrafts.

Scissors
Ask for a grown-up's help when using sharp scissors.

Pens
Write your labels with permanent marker.

Modeling clay
Works well as a base for your labels so they stand up.

Tape
Useful for sticking things down or creating guides for drawing.

Craft sticks
Use these to label your seeds so you know what is in the pot.

Kitchen garden

Fruits, vegetables, and herbs taste best when they are homegrown. Learn how to grow these tasty foods.

What is a kitchen garden?

A kitchen garden is anywhere you grow things to eat. It can be any size, from a small collection of containers to a large raised bed.

Vegetable patch
If you've got a large space in your yard, you can sow all sorts of things. The plants shown here are happy in most types of soil and can be planted in pots or in the ground outside.

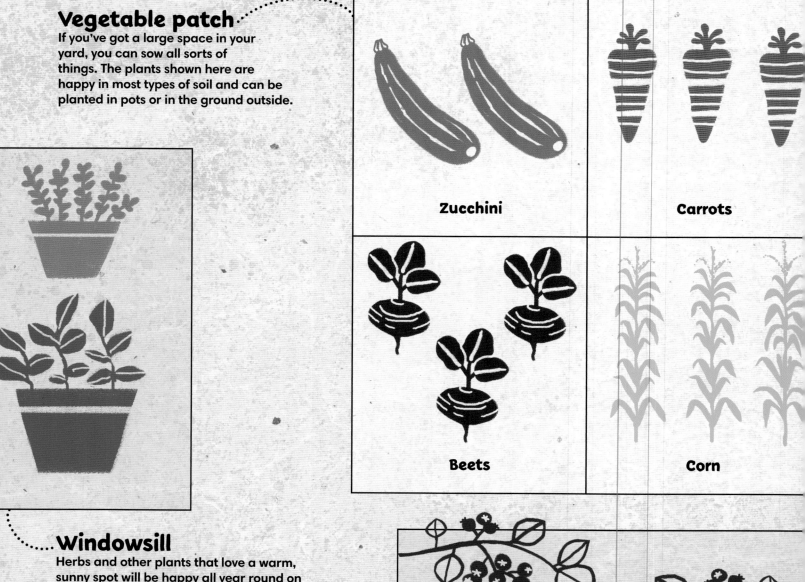

Zucchini

Carrots

Beets

Corn

Blueberries

Windowsill
Herbs and other plants that love a warm, sunny spot will be happy all year round on a windowsill. You can also grow seedlings to plant outdoors in the spring.

Stakes
Narrow spaces work well for plants that like to climb. Berries, such as raspberries, can be grown up stakes.

Trees
If you have the space, a fruit tree will provide fruit to eat year after year. How about planting an apple, pear, plum, or cherry tree?

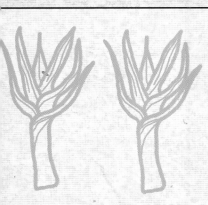

Leeks

Onions

Strawberries

Lemons

Pumpkins

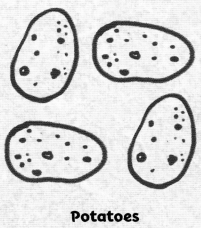

Potatoes

Pots and containers
Many plants like to get started in a container. You can grow your plants to a good size and then plant them outside in the soil. You can also leave them in their containers—it makes them much easier to move around!

Raised beds
A raised bed is a box made of wooden planks. You can fill it with any type of soil, so choose one that best suits the plants you want to grow.

Lettuce

Growing herbs

Herbs such as oregano, parsley, and thyme can easily be grown from seed. In winter, however, it's best to grow them on a sunny windowsill using potted herbs.

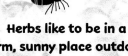

Herbs like to be in a warm, sunny place outdoors. A little shade is okay, but don't put them somewhere that is always shady.

You will need

Cartons

Scissors

Pen or pencil

Large paper clips

Stones

All-purpose compost

Paper or cardboard

Herb seeds

1

Collect a number of fruit juice cartons. These will make colorful containers for your herbs. They also have a waterproof lining and will not fall apart.

2

Using scissors, cut off the top quarter of the carton. Next, make drainage holes in the bottom using a pen or pencil.

3

Join your containers together with large paper clips. Arrange them in a pattern—they look best if you place the side with writing at the back.

4

Put a few stones at the bottom of each carton for drainage, then fill the cartons with all-purpose compost. It may be easier to do this if you make a cone out of paper or cardboard.

5

Sprinkle a few oregano, parsley, and thyme seeds into separate cartons. Cover with a thin layer of compost. Water the soil and leave the seeds in a well lit place to germinate. Keep the herbs lightly watered.

6

Thin out the seedlings if they get crowded. You can eat the little plants you've pulled out. Don't let your herbs dry out.

How to grow Carrots

You can grow all kinds of carrots—large ones, round ones, and different colored ones. The first wild carrots were purple, yellow, or white and tasted bitter. Over the centuries, however, gardeners have bred all colors of carrot to be sweet and juicy.

You will need

Burlap bag

Trash can liner

Stapler

Carrot seeds

Sand

Compost

Liquid fertilizer

You can keep carrots for months after you've dug them up. Trim off the leaves, then layer them in slightly damp sand, making sure they aren't touching.

1

2

3

Line a burlap bag with a trash can liner, stapled in place. Poke drainage holes in the bottom of the bag.

Carrot seeds are small, so you might want to mix them with a little sand so you can plant them evenly.

Fill your container with compost. Make shallow trenches. Thinly sprinkle the seeds in the trenches and cover them with more compost.

4

5

6

Thin out your carrots as they push through the soil by pulling out about half of the plants. Leave a gap of roughly 2 in (5 cm) between them.

Carrots need plenty of water as they grow. Add an all-purpose liquid fertilizer once a week when the leaves start to grow rapidly.

When the carrots are big enough to eat (around 12 weeks after planting), lift them from the compost. Wash them well before eating them!

How to Grow Potatoes

Potatoes are easy and fun to grow. Everyone loves eating them—as buttery baked potatoes, creamy mashed potatoes, fabulous fries, and crunchy chips.

You will need

Seed potatoes

Egg carton

Burlap sack

Trash can liner

Compost

Scissors

Don't plant more than four or five seed potatoes in your sack.

1

Put seed potatoes, with their sprouting "eyes" pointing up, in an empty egg carton. Leave them in a light, unheated place until they sprout.

2

Line a rolled-down burlap sack with a trash can liner. Make drainage holes in the bottom. Cover the potatoes in all-purpose compost, with the shoots pointing up.

3

When leaves grow, cover the stalks with compost and partly roll up the sack. This is called hilling. More potatoes will grow off the stalks.

4

Keep hilling as the plants grow. Unroll the bag and sack a little each time until they are fully unrolled.

5

The potatoes are ready for harvesting when the leaves begin to turn yellow. Cut the sack to get them out.

6

Remove the potatoes and leave them on the soil for a few hours to dry.

How to Grow Beets

There are white and yellow varieties of beet, but the most well-known color is a deep purple-red. Beets are yummy in salads or pickled in vinegar.

You will need

Container

Beet seeds

Soil

Garden fork

Don't put the plants too close together. The roots need space to grow.

1

Make holes 1 in (2.5 cm) deep in a large container. Sow two seeds into each hole, cover with soil, and water.

2

Thin the seedlings when they are 1 in (2.5 cm) high by taking out one of the seedlings from each hole.

3

Keep the plants well watered. Dry spells can cause the beets to become woody and split.

4

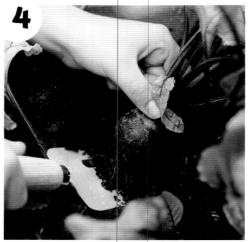

Pick when each beet is the size of a ping-pong ball. Lift the beet and use a garden fork to lever under the root.

Beet leaves can be eaten like spinach. Twist off the tops with your hands, rather than cutting with a knife.

How to Grow Lettuce

Flat or curly, green or purple, crispy lettuce leaves come in many varieties. Sow the seeds at any time throughout the spring and summer.

1

In a pot of seed compost, use a pencil to make a hole ½ in (1.5 cm) deep.

2

Take a pinch of lettuce seeds and sprinkle them in each hole in your pot.

You will need

Plant pots

Seed compost

Pencil

Lettuce seeds

Label

Gravel

3

Using your fingertips, cover the seeds with compost, then water. Label with the variety of lettuce.

4

Once the seedlings start to grow, pull some out to allow space for good growth.

5

When the plants have grown to this size, transfer each lettuce to its own pot. Pour gravel around the base to deter hungry slugs.

You can grow crops in a wooden crate. Line it with a trash can bag and fill with compost, then sow the seeds. The wood keeps in valuable warmth and moisture.

6

Water often to keep the soil moist. This needs to be done once or twice a day in warm weather.

7

Pick the outer leaves when you need them. Your lettuce will keep growing more leaves.

How to Grow
Leeks

Grown for more than 6,000 years, leeks are thought to have been eaten by the ancient Egyptians! Now you can grow these ancient vegetables, too.

Leeks hate competing with weeds, so make sure you keep the soil around them free of wild plants.

You will need

Small and large pots

Soil

Leek seeds

Scissors

Liquid plant food

Trowel

1

Fill pots with soil. Make a hole ½ in (1.5 cm) deep with your finger or a pencil and add a few leek seeds. Cover with soil, then water. You can keep your pots outdoors.

2

Once the seedlings are growing healthily, water them well. Make some holes 6 in (15 cm) deep in a large pot. Next, lift out the seedlings and carefully separate them.

3

Trim each leek's root ends to 1 in (2.5 cm) long with scissors. Place each one in its own hole in the large pot.

4

Fill each hole with water. The soil washed in will hold the leeks in place. Continue to water regularly, and use a liquid plant food once a month.

5

Get longer leeks by adding more soil to the pot, raising the soil level around the base of each leek.

6

Remove some baby leeks when small. Leave other leeks in longer—even over winter—to grow bigger.

How to Grow
Spinach

All parts of spinach plants have been cooked or used in medicines since ancient times. The tasty leaves and stalks help to keep us healthy and strong.

1

Plant seeds starting in mid spring. Using a ruler, measure a trench 1 in (2.5 cm) deep. Sow the seeds thinly.

2

Once they have germinated, thin the seedlings to 3 in (8 cm) apart. Thin them again later, if necessary.

You will need

Long container

Compost

Ruler

Spinach seeds

Liquid plant food

Fertilizer

Scissors

3

Keep well watered, use a liquid plant food once a month, and add a nitrogen-rich fertilizer to the soil.

4

Cut off flowering shoots. This will help the plant to produce better leaves.

5

Encourage new growth by picking a few leaves when they get longer than 2 in (5 cm).

Grow spinach in a cool place, out of direct sunlight.

How to Grow Chilies

Spicy chili peppers add zest to lots of recipes and taste delicious. They grow well in very warm spots with lots of sunlight. Grow them in the summer for the best results.

You will need

- Chili seeds
- Seed-starting pots
- Soil
- Medium pots
- Fertilizer

Cut the chili fruit off the plant rather than pulling. If the plant is outside, do this before the end of summer!

1 Sprinkle the seeds in starting pots full of soil. Cover the seeds with a thin layer of soil and keep them warm.

2 Once the seeds poke up through the soil (7 to 10 days after sowing), water them every couple of days.

3 When the plants are big enough, carefully move them into medium-size pots.

4 Put your plants in a sunny spot. Water every few days. Once fruit starts to appear, give them tomato plant food once a week.

Wash your hands after touching chilies, since they can sting your eyes.

How to Grow Eggplant

Eggplant evolved from a spiny plant from India that has a small, white egg-shaped fruit—which is where the eggplant got its name. In some countries, eggplant is known as aubergine.

You will need

Yogurt cup

Trowel

Seed compost

Eggplant seeds

Label

Container

Spray bottle

Liquid plant food

Stake

String

1

Make holes in the base of a clean yogurt cup and fill with seed compost. Make a hole about ¼ in (6 mm) deep in the compost.

2

Sow two seeds in the hole and brush soil over them. Add a label, water the seeds, and place the cup on a windowsill.

3

After the plants start sprouting, remove the smaller seedling to allow the other one more space to continue growing.

4

When spring comes, tip the plant out and place into a hole in a large container of soil. Pat the soil around the plant and water it.

5

Water little but often. If you have a greenhouse, your plant will flourish there.

6

Eggplant flowers are colorful, to attract insects for pollinating. Pollination allows the flowers to turn into eggplants.

7

Spray the fruits that develop from the flowers with water. As the fruits start to swell, add liquid plant food.

8

Once your plant has reached 12 in (30 cm) tall, pinch or snip off the growing stems at the top. This encourages the rest of the plant to grow. Tie your plant to a stake for support.

9

Pick each fruit when it is 4 in (10 cm) long and has a shine on its skin. You should get between five and 10 fruits within a few months.

How to Grow Zucchini

Zucchini are vegetables that can be many odd shapes, colors, and sizes. Why not grow a different variety each year?

1

Push two seeds on their sides into a ½ in (1.5 cm) deep hole in a pot of soil. Water, label, and place the seed pot on a windowsill.

2

Once the plants sprout, remove the weakest seedling and put the other one outside. Protect it with a covering made from a plastic bottle.

You will need

- Zucchini seeds
- Plant pot
- Soil
- Label
- Plastic bottle
- Liquid plant food
- Knife

3

When the roots begin to show through the bottom of the pot, tip the young plant out of its pot, supporting its stem.

4

Place the plant in a hole in a flowerbed, pat soil around it, and water.

5

The bright yellow flowers attract insects, which pollinate the flowers so they can become fruit.

Zucchini are young squash plants. You can leave a few attached to grow into giant summer squash, which can be twice as big as zucchini.

6

Water the soil around the plant rather than straight onto it, as this can cause the plant to rot. Give it some liquid plant food.

7

Pick the flower from the tip of the growing zucchini. These can be cooked and eaten.

8

Cut the zucchini at their base when they reach 4 in (10 cm). Ask an adult to help you with the knife.

How to Grow Pumpkins

These large, heavy fruits belong to the squash family. Although some squashes grow quickly, pumpkins can take a long time to ripen.

You will need

Plant pot

Soil

Pumpkin seed

Large container

Stakes

String

Plant food

Netting

Mulch

Knife

Pumpkins are one of nature's biggest vegetables. Record-breaking pumpkins can weigh more than 1,000 lb (450 kg)!

1

In spring, make a ½ in (1.5 cm) deep hole in a pot of soil. Sow one seed on its side, cover with soil, water, and put on a windowsill.

2

Keep well watered. Your plant is ready to transplant once the roots poke out of the bottom of the pot.

3

Make a hole in a large container of soil. Carefully place the plant into the hole. Pat soil around it and water.

4

Wrap and tie the stem around four stakes. As the stem grows, keep wrapping and tying it to the stakes.

5

Keep the soil well watered. Your plant will produce flowers, attracting insects to pollinate.

6

Feed your plant with plant food every few weeks once the fruits start to form.

7

Make a net hammock to support fruit growing above the ground. Attach the hammock to two of the stakes.

8

Add mulch around fruit growing on the ground. Keep turning the fruit slightly to ripen evenly.

9

Cut the fruit off once it has fully matured. Ask an adult to help you cut it and lift it.

How to Grow Beans

Green beans or scarlet runner beans? Snap, string, wax, or bush beans? You'll have a tough time deciding which beans to grow!

1 Push four stakes into a large pot of soil and tie them together at the top.

2 Plant the beans 2 in (5 cm) deep on each side of a stake. Cover with soil, then water and label.

You will need

- Stakes
- Plant pot
- Soil
- Beans
- Label
- Straw or mulch
- Liquid plant food

3 Wind each seedling around a stake. It will grow up it. Cover the soil with straw or mulch.

4 Squirt off any aphids (small green insects) with water. Keep watering the soil often, and use a liquid plant food every two weeks.

5 Pick the bean pods when they are long but still tender. Pick often, so that new beans will grow.

Since ancient times, beans have been eaten as a good source of protein.

How to grow Peppers

Next time you buy bell peppers, don't throw away the seeds—plant them instead. Choose fresh orange or red bell peppers for your seeds, as these are most likely to grow.

1

Cut open your bell pepper, then use the handle of a spoon to gently push out the seeds.

2

Wash the seeds in water to get rid of a natural anti-germinating substance that stops the seeds from growing inside the fruit.

You will need

Ripe bell pepper

Knife

Spoon

Pots

Seed compost

Grow-bag compost

Tomato fertilizer

Mulch

3

Plant your seeds about ¼ in (6 mm) deep in pots filled with seed compost.

4

When the plants fill their pots, plant them in large containers of grow-bag compost. Feed with tomato fertilizer every two weeks.

5

Water regularly. To keep the compost damp, cover it with mulch, as this helps hold in the moisture.

Plant watch

The bell peppers you grow may not look like your original pepper! Many supermarket peppers are hybrids (plants whose parents were different varieties), so their offspring may take after only one of the parents.

How to grow Corn

If you grow your own corn, you can pick it and cook it or eat it straight off the plant. This is when it is sweetest. You can also grow corn to make popcorn.

1

Corn is a tall cereal grass with long ears full of starchy seeds. Its seeds are the dried kernels of corn on the cob.

2

Sow the seeds about ½ in (1.5 cm) deep in compost. Water regularly and keep in a warm place until the seeds start to sprout.

You will need

Dried corn kernel seeds

Compost

Containers

Cardboard

Grow-bag compost

Tomato fertilizer

Stakes

3

Once the leaves appear, start putting your plants outside in the sun for a few hours each day.

4

Corn has long roots, so choose a large container. Cover any holes with cardboard or plastic bags with drainage holes.

5

Plant in grow-bag compost, without disturbing the roots. Stand your plants in full sun and keep them well watered.

Corn is pollinated by the wind. The female flowers are the silks, the long parts that hang out of the ear of corn to catch pollen blown by the wind from another plant. Each pollinated silk becomes one kernel of corn.

6

If roots appear on the surface, cover them with compost. Feed with tomato fertilizer every two weeks.

7

Support your plants on stakes as they grow. The ears are ready to test when the silks turn brown.

43

How to Grow Tomatoes

Even when you are short on space, you can still grow an impressive pot of little tomatoes. The tomatoes shown here are a type called Supersweet 100, but there are lots of varieties to choose from.

You will need

- Containers
- Seed compost
- Seeds
- Hammer and nail
- Tape
- All-purpose compost

When tiny fruits begin to appear, feed the plants with tomato food to help them ripen.

1

Fill a pot with seed compost. Sprinkle seeds onto the compost and cover with ¼ in (6 mm) more compost.

2

Keep the seeds in a warm place. When the seedlings start to grow, move to a sunny position.

3

Ask an adult to use a hammer and nail to make drainage holes in a container. Tape stops the nail from slipping.

4

Transplant two or three plants into all-purpose compost. Be careful not to disturb the roots.

5

Firm the compost around the plants, making sure all the roots are covered.

6

Put the plants back in their sunny spot and keep them well watered as they grow.

How to grow Blueberries

Blueberry bushes grow well in pots filled with acidic, or ericaceous, soil. Care for them year after year, and you'll be rewarded with lots of fruit.

You will need

- Large pot
- Compost
- Blueberry plant
- Mulch
- Netting
- Rainwater

Blueberry bushes grow best in a mixture of ericaceous compost and peat.

1 Fill your pot with compost and carefully drop in your blueberry plant. Press down more compost around the plant.

2 Mulch around the new plant using bark or pine needles, which are fairly acidic. Do this again each spring.

3 If your new plant already has some berries, cover it with netting to stop birds from eating the berries.

4 Water the new plant well from spring to fall. Use rainwater, because tap water will make the soil less acidic.

Blueberries form in clusters, but ripen at different times. Pick each berry a few days after it turns a deep blue color.

How to Grow Strawberries

Follow the steps below and you will have delicious red strawberries to enjoy eating in the summer, year after year.

1

Start off with a strawberry plug. The neat root ball makes the plug easy to plant and quick to grow.

2

Place the plug in a medium pot of soil. The top of the roots should be level with the soil. Water well.

You will need

Strawberry plug

Medium pot

Soil

Straw

Plant food

There are about 200 seeds on the outer skin of each strawberry.

3

Put straw under the plant to prevent the strawberries from touching the ground.

4

Water every day. Once the plant starts flowering, give it liquid plant food every 10 days.

5

Check to see if any strawberries have turned red. As soon as one is ripe, pick right away. Water often as the strawberries begin to swell.

Cover your plant with netting if birds are eating the strawberries.

49

How to Grow Lemons

A lemon tree needs year-round care to produce lots of lemons. Cover your tree in winter and feed it every month from early spring to late summer.

You will need

- Lemon seeds or young lemon tree
- Pots
- Trowel
- Citrus compost
- Mulch

Growing from seed

Lemon seed

Cut a lemon in half and remove the seeds.

Select the undamaged seeds. Sow them while they are still moist.

Have patience! It's likely to take many years before your fruit grows.

Growing from a young tree

1

Choose a lemon tree that is ready to begin fruiting. Place it upright in a pot filled with citrus compost.

2

Add 2 in (5 cm) mulch around the trunk to keep in moisture and water often to begin with.

3

As the tree grows, water only when the topsoil looks dry. During the winter, the tree will need less water.

Lemons contain the most vitamin C of any citrus fruit. In the past, sailors ate them on voyages to stay healthy.

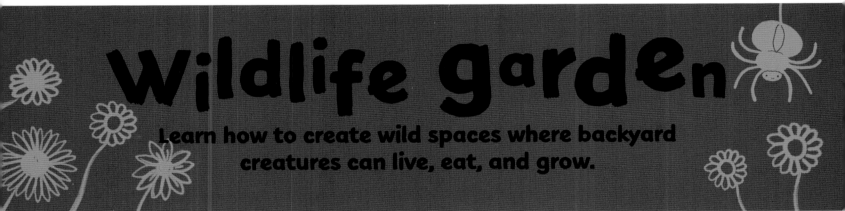

Wildlife garden

Learn how to create wild spaces where backyard creatures can live, eat, and grow.

Why be a wildlife gardener?

It is so exciting to see animals flourish in a beautiful garden YOU created. Creatures will visit your garden with a little encouragement, and they will work hard to keep your garden healthy.

Pest control

Lots of creatures can damage your garden, but by providing a home for a variety of wildlife you can create a natural balance. Ladybugs love to eat aphids, spiders catch mosquitoes in their webs, and chickadees devour caterpillars.

Flower power

Bees and butterflies are pollinators. This means they transfer pollen (fine grains) from flower to flower, so seeds are made and the next generation of plants can grow. Without them, many flowering plants would not exist.

Sow the seed

Animals help to spread seeds far and wide. Many seeds are found inside tasty fruit. After animals have eaten the fruit, these seeds are spread in their droppings.

It's fun!

Watching birds on a feeder, a squirrel darting across the lawn, or newts diving in a pond is even more satisfying if you know you helped to provide and protect their homes.

Super worms

Worms make the soil healthy for growing plants. These incredible creatures eat decaying plant matter, making room for new plants. Worm poop is full of nutrients that the plants need to grow.

Your garden is a habitat

Wildlife can be big, small, or microscopic. It can live in water, soil, or in the branches of a tree. From the cutest mammal to the wriggliest bug, animals need each other. Turning your garden and yard into a haven for wildlife means letting all animals thrive.

Food web
Here's a food web that might exist in anyone's garden. Remember, even the creatures you may not like provide food for other animals.

Too few birds could mean too many snails and caterpillars! Upsetting the balance of a wildlife garden can have disastrous effects on the plants.

Ladybugs do a good job eating aphids—a garden pest that attacks plants.

Birds eat the worms that feed on rotten apples.

Ants, worms, and snails break down dead matter so that it enters the soil and provides nutrients that feed plants.

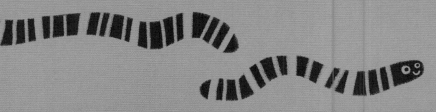

Green corridor

You may think a small, city garden will not make much difference to wildlife populations, but a row of neighboring yards provides a large habitat. These so-called "green corridors" in cities are spied out by migrating birds and used as an area to rest as they fly across big cities.

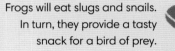

Top predators such as a fox or owl will keep rodents in check. A variety of prey and predators keeps the food chain in balance.

Frogs will eat slugs and snails. In turn, they provide a tasty snack for a bird of prey.

Butterflies, moths, and bees live off the nectar in flowers. They become a meal for a frog or bird.

Nature SOS

It is up to us to help preserve nature, but, all too often, human beings act more like its attackers. The decline in numbers of creatures such as stag beetles, house sparrows, bees, and many types of moths and butterflies can be slowed down, and even halted, if we all do our part.

Your seasonal Wildlife garden

The wildlife in your garden and yard varies with the seasons. Spot baby animals in spring. Summer is abuzz with wildlife. Fall is a time of feast and plenty for wildlife. Many animals hibernate in winter.

Spring

Wake up! It's springtime. Animals such as frogs, toads, newts, dormice, and spiders wake up from hibernation. Birds make nests and lay eggs, while frogs and toads release their spawn into ponds.

Summer

The warm, sunny days mean lots of food. Butterflies flit between flowers, fledgling birds take to the air, and bees work tirelessly to produce honey. Baby frogs and toads can be spotted in ponds.

Hibernation log pile

A log pile is a welcome place for animals and insects looking for somewhere to hibernate. Build this log pile in an undisturbed corner and leave it alone until spring.

1

2

3

Dig a shallow pit in a place that won't be disturbed. Pile up the logs, with the biggest logs at the bottom.

Pile up the smaller sticks on top. Fill any spaces with things such as bark, pine cones, and leaves.

Plant ivy and trail it over the log pile. This provides even more cover for little animals.

Fall

In the fall, a feast of berries and fruit attracts birds trying to fatten up before winter. Squirrels bury nuts to eat later. Some creatures are looking for a place to sleep out the winter.

Winter

Some animals sleep through the winter, but others stay awake. This is the season when they most need our help. Birds are vulnerable and need high-energy food and water to survive the cold months ahead.

A Wildlife hedge

Hedges are alive with wildlife. They provide food and shelter, as well as a place for animals to hibernate and raise their young. Hedge flowers attract buzzing bees, butterflies, and other bugs.

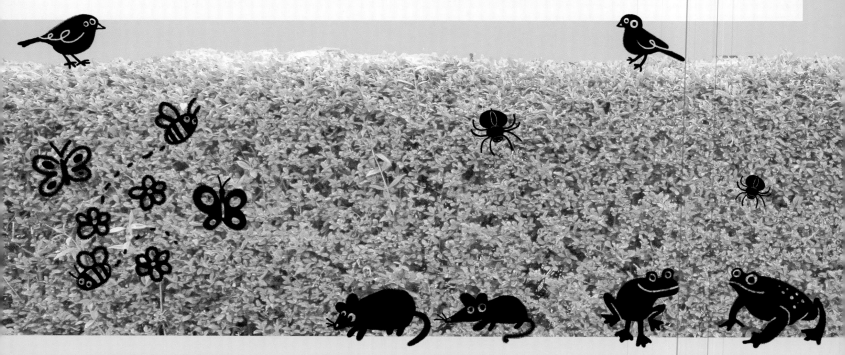

Bees and butterflies
are attracted by the flowers that grow on some hedges, like privet and hawthorn.

Mice
are agile and can climb to the upper branches of hedges. They are on the lookout for snails, centipedes, and other tasty creatures.

Frogs and toads
hibernate (sleep through the winter) in old wood that gathers at the bottom of the hedge.

Grow your own hedge

If you don't have much space, you can grow a mini hedge in a long, wide container full of all-purpose compost. Place the plants close to each other and let them knit together. Prune to manage the height. Your hedge will soon attract lots of pollinators.

Plant your hedge trees and shrubs in the fall for best results.

Voles shelter at the bottom of a hedge and use its protection to move from one part of the garden to another. These shy creatures like to stay hidden.

Birds make their nests in hedges and eat the nuts and berries of plants—or any bugs they may find there.

Insects feed and live on plants. Bugs also make a tasty snack for birds. Many are well camouflaged to blend into their green background!

Plants for a fragrant Garden

A garden is not just pretty to look at—if you choose the right plants, your garden can surround you with sweet smells all year round. The perfume comes from oils stored in the flower's petals that are released as it opens.

Scent signals

Flowers produce strong scents to attract the insects and birds that pollinate them. When flowers smell nice, animals know there is pollen and nectar inside. Pollen clings to the animals' feet and bodies when they land on blooms, and they carry the pollen to the next flower. But not all flowers smell sweet—some have a horrible scent to attract flies! Some plants only open and release their scent at night. They do this to attract night-flying pollinators, such as moths and bats.

Orchids

Orchids range in smell, from fruity to spicy.

Rose

The classic rose fragrance is one of the best-loved scents. There are lots of different types of rose. They come in a range of colors, and some have petals that are particularly thick and velvety.

Honeysuckle

Honeysuckle is a strong climber that is easy to grow. The vine produces bright flowers during the summer. Plant it in the ground, then train it up a trellis.

Jasmine

This plant has delicately scented white blooms.

Freesia

A spring flower, freesia has a powerful scent.

Nicotiana

Nicotiana blooms—also known as flowering tobacco—open and release their powerful fragrance when the sun goes down. Nicotiana likes moist, fertile soil and is happiest growing in partial shade.

Lavender

Lavender is a classic scented flower. It is native to North Africa and the area around the Mediterranean Sea, but is now loved all over the world.

Starting plants for wildlife

So, you've got a patio, backyard, or garden, and you want to start wildlife gardening. What should you plant? There are thousands of plants to choose from, and here's our top eight. This mixture of flowers, trees, climbers, and shrubs will make an ideal basis for your wildlife garden.

1 Wildflowers

Wildlife absolutely loves to eat wildflowers. Choose plants that grow naturally in your area.

- Sunny or partly shaded location
- Well drained, moist soil
- Grows 24 in (60 cm) high

2 Clematis
(C. tangutica)

Any type of clematis is popular with wildlife, and this variety is a climber that is bushy enough for birds to nest in.

- Sunny location
- Well drained soil
- Grows 22 ft (7 m) high

3 Dog rose
(Rosa canina)

This climbing rose has stunning pink flowers and the branches are clothed in beautiful red rosehip fruit in the fall.

- Sunny or partly shaded location
- Well drained, moist soil
- Grows 9 ft (3 m) high

4 Long grass

Grass that has been left to grow long will do wonders for wildlife. Birds use material for nests, insects will use it as cover, and ladybugs will hibernate in long tufts.

- Sunny or partly shaded location
- Well drained soil
- Grows 39 in (1 m) high

5 Common ivy
(Hedera helix)

An evergreen climber, ivy can be grown against walls or fences, where it will provide shelter and cover for birds.

- Sunny or partly shaded location
- Well drained, moist soil
- Grows 33 ft (10 m) high

6 French lavender
(Lavandula stoechas)

Bees and butterflies love the showy, scented flowers that top this evergreen. In summer, its leaves have a scent, too.

- Sunny location
- Well drained soil
- Grows 24 in (60 cm) high

7 Birch tree
(Betula pendula 'Youngii')

Young's birch has a weeping shape. It is a good choice for smaller gardens because it is fairly narrow.

- Sunny or partly shaded location
- Well drained, moist soil
- Grows 26 ft (8 m) high

8 Mixed native hedge

Native plants are ones that grow naturally in your area. This means your local animals will be used to them. Mixed native shrubs and trees provide nesting sites for birds, flowers for insects, and berries or nuts that will be eaten by many creatures.

- Sunny or partly shaded location
- Well drained, moist soil
- Grows 3–6 ft (1–2 m) high

Sunflowers

Sunflowers are great for wildlife! These plants are not only easy and fun to grow, reaching amazing heights, but they also provide year-round food for wildlife.

You will need

- Sunflower seeds
- Yogurt cups
- Seed compost
- Polyethylene
- Big pot
- Garden twine
- Stake

Prevent your sunflower from toppling over by securing stems to a stake with garden twine.

1 Plant seeds in yogurt cups full of seed compost. Sow a single seed in each, 1 in (2.5 cm) deep. Water.

2 Put in a sunny place and cover with polyethylene. Remove the covering when little shoots appear.

3 When your sunflower outgrows the yogurt cup, plant it in a big container with a drainage hole in the bottom.

4 Place your plant in a sunny spot outdoors when there is no risk of frost. Now, watch it grow.

Sunflowers provide nectar for bugs and a feast of seeds. Once the plant has flowered, let the head droop. Watch as small animals munch away at the seeds.

Mini nature Preserve

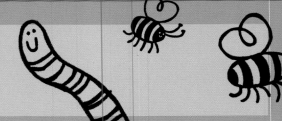

You don't need a big yard to attract wildlife. Plant a window box, or even an empty ice cream tub, and watch as the creepy-crawlies pay a visit!

You will need

- Window box
- Broken pots
- Compost
- Trowel
- Herbs
- Trailing plants
- Water
- Gravel or bark
- Pine cone
- Saucer or jar lid

Go local! Choose plenty of plants that grow naturally in your area—these will attract the most species of wildlife.

1

Make sure the window box has holes in the bottom. Cover the holes with broken pots.

2

Fill your window box with compost. Then plan where you'll be positioning the plants.

3

Plant the herbs and trailing plants. Water them well.

4

Fill the top with gravel or bark to prevent water loss. Add a pine cone to make a home for visiting bugs.

Include a shallow saucer of water and keep it filled. Wildlife can use it to drink or wash.

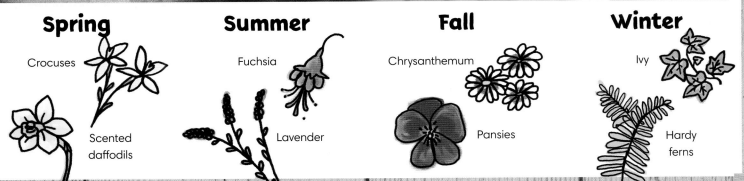

For a year-round nature preserve, choose plants that will attract bugs throughout the seasons. Here are some suggestions:

Spring

Crocuses

Scented daffodils

Summer

Fuchsia

Lavender

Fall

Chrysanthemum

Pansies

Winter

Ivy

Hardy ferns

Plant a tree

Every wildlife refuge should have a tree. Leafy canopies provide shelter for many creatures, while birds and small mammals build nests in trees and eat their berries, fruits, and nuts.

1

First, dig a hole. Make the hole twice as wide as the tree's root ball, the tangled mass of roots at the bottom of the trunk.

2

Check the depth by placing a stick across the hole. It should be level with the tree's container.

You will need

Shovel

Tree

Stick

Hammer

Stake

Rubber tree tie

Water

3

Remove the plastic around the tree's roots and fill in the soil around the tree.

4

Ask an adult to hammer in your stake at an angle. Tie the tree to the stake.

5

Job done! Keep the tree well watered. Remove the stake when the tree is strong enough to stand on its own.

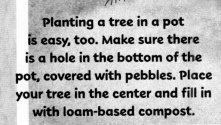

Planting a tree in a pot is easy, too. Make sure there is a hole in the bottom of the pot, covered with pebbles. Place your tree in the center and fill in with loam-based compost.

Water Plants

Pond plants keep the water healthy and clear, and they provide hiding places for animals. Here are some plants that thrive in ponds.

Oxygenating plants These help to stop the water from becoming murky.

1

Hornwort
(Ceratophyllum demersum)
This bristly plant spends most of its life underwater, but the stems float to the surface during summer.

- Sunny or lightly shaded location
- Wet soil
- Needs 35 in (90 cm) water depth

2

Hair grass
(Eleocharis acicularis)
This carpeting plant, which resembles grass, stays underwater all the time.

- Sunny or lightly shaded location
- Wet soil
- Needs 35 in (90 cm) water depth

Deep water plants These help to keep the pond cool.

1

Water hawthorn
(Aponogeton distachyos)
This pretty plant appears above the surface from early spring to fall.

- Sunny or partly shaded location
- Wet soil
- Needs 11–35 in (30–90 cm) water depth

2

Golden club
(Orontium aquaticum)
In spring, the golden club breaks the surface of the water with its oval leaves.

- Sunny or partly shaded location
- Wet soil
- Needs 17 in (45 cm) water depth

You'll need a mix of these four types of pond plants to make a healthy pond.

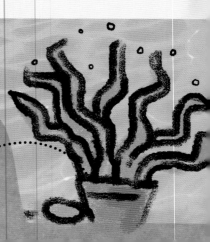

Oxygenating plants grow below the surface, giving off oxygen bubbles.

Floating plants These provide surface cover and stop the water from turning green.

1

Frogbit
(Hydrocharis morsus-ranae)
Frogbit forms a mass of rounded leaves that float on the surface.

- ☀ Sunny location
- 💧 Wet soil
- 📏 Short floater

2

Water lettuce
(Stratiotes aloides)
Dragonflies perch on water lettuce and eat the bugs it attracts. This plant is best suited for large ponds.

- ☀ Sunny location
- 💧 Wet soil
- 📏 Short floater

3

Common bladderwort
(Utricularia vulgaris)
This carnivorous plant has tiny air-filled sacs on its stems. When a bug touches the sac, it opens and water rushes in, taking the creature with it.

- ☀ Sunny location
- 💧 Wet soil
- 📏 Short floater

Marginals These provide safe havens for pond creatures.

1

Water forget-me-not
(Myosotis scorpiodes)
From late spring until the beginning of summer, this plant is covered in tiny blue flowers.

- ⛅ Sunny or partly shaded location
- 💧 Wet soil
- 📏 Grows 17 in (45 cm) high

2

Branched bur-reed
(Sparganium erectum)
This reed has narrow leaves that hide the flowering stems. The flowers become tiny seed heads in fall.

- ⛅ Sunny or partly shaded location
- 💧 Wet soil
- 📏 Grows 39 in (100 cm) high

3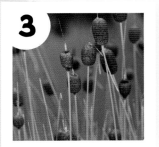

Dwarf cattail
(Typha minima)
The cattail's shoots grow like upright spears. The thin spike holds a brown seed head about the size of an acorn.

- ⛅ Sunny or partly shaded location
- 💧 Wet soil
- 📏 Grows 24 in (60 cm) high

Floating plants may have roots hanging free in the water.

Deep water plants are placed on or near the bottom of the pond.

Marginal plants grow in pots in the water around the pond.

Pond life

Like us, animals need to drink water and they like to bathe. Even a very small pond will quickly become alive with water bugs and other aquatic creatures.

Collect rainwater to top off the pond in hot weather.

You will need

Large plastic container

Sand

Shovel

Flat stones

Gravel

Bricks or stones

Water plants

Rainwater

1

Mark out the pond's boundary by trickling sand around the edges of your plastic container.

2

Dig around the edge of the boundary first, then dig out the middle, making a hole deep enough for the container.

3

Place the container into the hole so the top is level with the ground. Fill any gaps with soil.

4

Cover the edge of the pond with the flat stones. Cover the bottom with gravel, then put in bricks or stones to make different levels within the pond.

5

Take the water plants and cover their soil with gravel to stop them from floating away. Position the pots inside the pond.

6

Fill the pond with rainwater and add free-floating pond weed. Make a ramp for creatures to climb in and out by covering a piece of wood with wire mesh.

Pond dipping

Ponds are fascinating places to explore and are full of wildlife. In this watery world, you will find many unusual and bizarre-looking creatures. You can find wildlife in ponds and streams, but always be careful and go with an adult, because water can be hazardous.

What will you find?

Slowly sweep your net through the water. Turn the net inside out into a container that is half-filled with water. Take a close look and see what you can identify. Below are some animals often found in ponds.

IMPORTANT:
Always return the creatures you have caught to the same part of the pond.

Tadpole, the young of frogs and toads

Mosquito larvae swim just beneath the water or hang upside down just below the surface.

Pond skaters glide effortlessly across the surface of the pond. Look out for their darting movements.

Pond snails
look like their land relatives but eat pond plants and rotting plants.

Freshwater leeches
are flattened, wormlike creatures that are eaten by fish and insect larvae.

Damselfly nymphs
have ravenous appetites and look fearsome.

A **water beetle larvae** is a fierce carnivore. Don't touch! It has powerful jaws and sharp fangs.

Make sure to dip through areas with weeds because many animals hide in them.

Container pond

This mini pond will fit on a patio or balcony. Put it in a shady spot and make it where you want it to stay, so you don't have to move it when it's full of water.

You will need

Clean bricks

Gravel

Large container

Rainwater

Aquatic plants

Clothespin basket

Burlap sack

Soil

Fish (optional)

Put a stick in your pond as an escape route for small creatures that fall in!

Fill and top off your pond with rainwater, since tap water can kill fish. If you do have to use tap water, let it stand for a few days before adding your fish.

1

Arrange clean bricks and gravel in the bottom of the container. Fill two-thirds full with rainwater.

2

Put the oxygenating plants in first. Check the labels, as some plants need to be anchored, while others float freely in the water.

3

Stand marginal plants on the bricks at the edge of the pond. Leave these in their pots, but put a layer of gravel on the soil to keep it in place.

4

You can group marginal plants like marsh marigold and primrose. Line a clothespin basket with burlap, fill with soil, plant your plants, and top with gravel.

5

Fill the container with water, then put in one or two floating plants. Some of the water surface should be left clear of plants.

6

Now add your fish! Small goldfish or mosquito fish are perfect for mini ponds. Move fish to a larger container as they grow.

Make a frog and toad home

Frogs and toads make great backyard residents. They gobble up many creatures that we consider pests, so make them feel welcome by building them a special home.

1

Dig out a hole a bit longer than the clay pot, in a cool, moist place in the shade.

2

Place the pot on its side in the hole. Bury about half of it by filling the inside with some soil.

You will need

Trowel

Clay pot

Soil

Damp leaves

Water

Saucer

Gravel

3

Use some damp leaves to make a nice bed for the frog or toad inside the pot.

4

Moisten the area with a little water to keep the pot in place.

5

Place a saucer of gravel and water nearby for the frog or toad to splash around in.

Frogs and toads like cool, damp, shallow burrows to hide out in and to hibernate in during the winter.

Frog Lodge

Plants for bees

Bees are the ultimate pollen and nectar collectors! Plant some of these top ten plants for bees and soon your garden will be buzzing with life.

1 Thyme
(Thymus citriodorus)
Throughout the summer, this herb is covered with tiny pink flowers that are a great favorite with bees.

☀ Sunny location
💧 Well drained soil
📏 Grows 12 in (30 cm) high

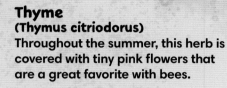

2 Heathers
(Calluna and Erica)
Heathers are bushes that come in many different shapes, sizes, and colors. Some flower in winter, so choose summer-flowering varieties for the bees.

☀ Sunny location
💧 Acidic, well drained soil
📏 Grows 12 in (30 cm) high

3 Purple sage
(Salvia officinalis 'Purpurascens')
Purple sage has pretty purple leaves that are edible. Bees love the bluish flowers that appear in summer.

☀ Sunny location
💧 Well drained, moist soil
📏 Grows 31 in (80 cm) high

4 Sunflowers
(Helianthus annuus)
These yellow flowers follow the sun as it moves across the sky. Bees love their luscious nectar.

☀ Sunny location
💧 Well drained, moist soil
📏 Grows 8 ft (2.5 m) high

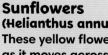
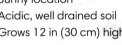

5 Honeysuckle
(Lonicera varieties)
There are lots of different types of honeysuckle, ranging from white to bright red. This climber is fantastic for feeding the bees in summer.

☀ Sunny location
💧 Well drained, moist soil
📏 Grows 22 ft (7 m) high

6 Verbena
(Verbena bonariensis)
Verbena has a long, wiry stem with a purple pompom of flowers at the end. It flowers over a long period, from late spring to the first frosts.

☀ Sunny location
💧 Well drained, moist soil
📏 Grows 59 in (150 cm) high

7 Meadow cranesbill
(Geranium pratense)
Meadow cranesbill has large, saucer-shaped, purplish flowers that sit above mounds of foliage in early summer.

⛅ Sunny or partly shaded location
💧 Well drained, moist soil
📏 Grows 23 in (60 cm) high

8 English lavender
(Lavandula angustifolia)
With its silvery, evergreen leaves and gorgeous, scented spikes of purple flowers, lavender bushes are always abuzz with nectar drinkers.

☀ Sunny location
💧 Well drained, moist soil
📏 Grows 39 in (1 m) high

9 Hollyhocks
(Alcea rosea)
Almost as tall as a sunflower, a hollyhock really shoots up! Its stems are studded with lots of large flowers, which appear from early- to mid-summer.

☀ Sunny location
💧 Well drained soil
📏 Grows 5-8 ft (1.5-2.5m) high

10 Borage
(Borago officinalis)
This plant will spread quickly around the garden. It has clumps of bristly leaves and bright blue flowers all summer long.

⛅ Sunny or partly shaded location
💧 Well drained soil
📏 Grows 23 in (60 cm) high

create a bee hotel

Buzzing bees make the yard a lively place as they busily pollinate our favorite plants from spring to fall. Attract bees by planting flowers and providing nesting sites.

You will need

Bamboo stakes

Tape

Scissors

Modeling clay

Clay pot

Some solitary bees make their nests in hollow plant stems or holes and cracks in bricks and wood. To create an alternative bee hotel, ask an adult to drill 6 in (15 cm) deep holes, ¼ in (6–10 mm) wide, into a piece of untreated wood.

1

Stand the pieces of bamboo on end to make a bundle. Then bind them together with tape.

2

Press the bundle into a lump of modeling clay to seal off one end.

3

Put the stakes into the pot, open ends facing out. Use more clay to wedge the bundle tightly inside the pot.

4

Leave the pot on its side in a sunny, dry spot where solitary bees can find it and stay for a while.

Fossils show that bees first appeared on Earth 150 million years ago.

What bee did I see?

There are about 40,000 different species of bee in the world. There are only seven species that make honey, which makes them very special. These bees live together in hives, but over 90% of bees are solitary and like to live alone.

Honey bee   Bumble bee   Mining bee

Ladybug Sanctuary

Ladybugs are a gardener's best friend. Although small, these spotted creatures have a ravenous appetite for aphids and other tiny pests that cause damage to plants.

You will need

- Plastic bottle
- Scissors
- Corrugated cardboard
- Twigs

A single ladybug can eat up to 5,000 aphids in its lifetime.

1 Ask an adult to cut the top off a plastic bottle. Next, cut out a piece of corrugated cardboard about the length of the bottle.

2 Roll the cardboard up tightly. Place the rolled-up cardboard into the plastic bottle.

3 Fill the hole with twigs for the ladybugs to land on. Place the bottle in a dry, sheltered spot.

4 The bottom of the bottle needs to be higher than the opening to allow water to drain away.

The spottiest ladybugs have 24 spots on their backs.

Hibernation

Ladybugs often use the same site to hibernate (sleep through the winter) every year, and they sometimes hibernate in colonies of hundreds of ladybugs. It is thought that they release a scent to attract others, since huddling together helps them keep warm.

Plants for caterpillars and butterflies

Caterpillars are fussy eaters, so butterflies lay their eggs only on plants that their hungry offspring will eat. Once the caterpillars transform into butterflies, they often seek out plants with nectar-filled flowers.

Plants for caterpillars

1 Nettles
(Urtica dioica)
A patch of nettles is the favorite plant of red admiral, peacock, and small tortoiseshell butterflies.

- Sunny or lightly shaded location
- Moist soil
- Grows 5 ft (1.5 m) high

2 Bird's foot trefoil
(Lotus corniculatus)
This pretty yellow wildflower with red tips is loved by the caterpillars of many types of butterfly.

- Sunny location
- Well drained soil
- Grows 11 in (30 cm) high

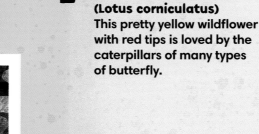

3 Nasturtium
(Tropaeolum)
The caterpillars of the small and large cabbage white butterflies love to munch on nasturtiums.

- Sunny location
- Well drained soil
- Grows 11 in–10 ft (30 cm–3 m) high

4 Garlic mustard
(Alliaria petiolata)
Green-veined white butterflies and orange-tip butterflies lay eggs on this plant. Its leaves smell of garlic.

- Sunny or partly shaded location
- Wet soil
- Grows 39 in (1 m) high

Plants for butterflies

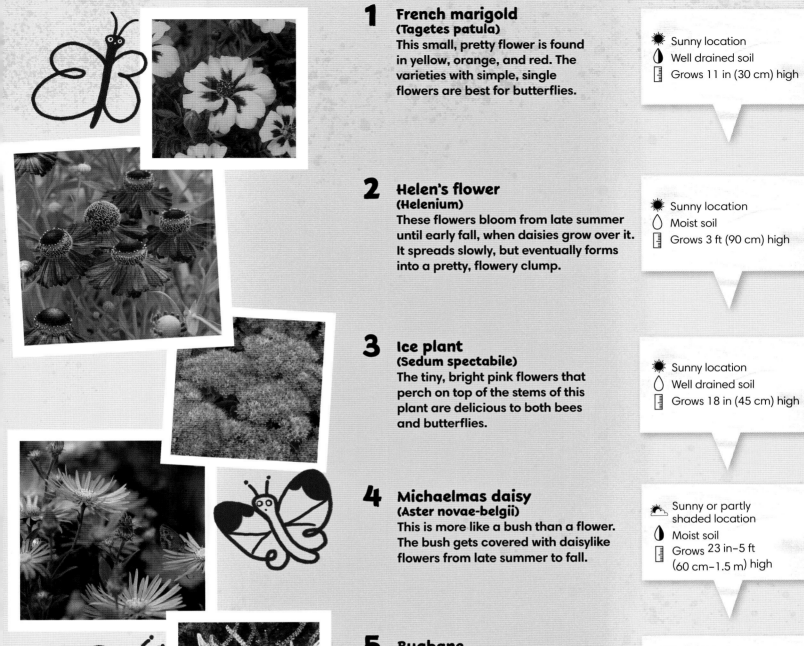

1 French marigold
(Tagetes patula)
This small, pretty flower is found in yellow, orange, and red. The varieties with simple, single flowers are best for butterflies.

- ☀ Sunny location
- ◊ Well drained soil
- ▤ Grows 11 in (30 cm) high

2 Helen's flower
(Helenium)
These flowers bloom from late summer until early fall, when daisies grow over it. It spreads slowly, but eventually forms into a pretty, flowery clump.

- ☀ Sunny location
- ◊ Moist soil
- ▤ Grows 3 ft (90 cm) high

3 Ice plant
(Sedum spectabile)
The tiny, bright pink flowers that perch on top of the stems of this plant are delicious to both bees and butterflies.

- ☀ Sunny location
- ◊ Well drained soil
- ▤ Grows 18 in (45 cm) high

4 Michaelmas daisy
(Aster novae-belgii)
This is more like a bush than a flower. The bush gets covered with daisylike flowers from late summer to fall.

- ☀☁ Sunny or partly shaded location
- ◊ Moist soil
- ▤ Grows 23 in–5 ft (60 cm–1.5 m) high

5 Bugbane
(Cimicifuga simplex)
Bugbane is a great nectar provider, especially in fall when butterflies are running out of summer flowers.

- ☀☁ Sunny or partly shaded location
- ◊ Moist soil
- ▤ Grows 4 ft (1.2 m) high

6 Hyssop
(Hyssopus officinalis)
This evergreen herb has bluish flowers that last throughout summer and into early fall, providing a summer feast for butterflies.

- ☀ Sunny location
- ◊ Well drained soil
- ▤ Grows 23 in (60 cm) high

Butterfly feeder

Beautiful butterflies love to eat sweet things, like the nectar from flowers or very ripe fruit. You can make them a delicious dinner using just an overripe banana.

You will need

- Very ripe banana
- Dinner knife
- Pen or pencil
- Construction paper
- Scissors
- Stickers
- Glue
- Lollipop sticks

If you have a whole bunch of overripe bananas, use the rest to bake some banana bread.

1

Leave a banana in the fruit bowl for a week, until it gets brown spots. Mash it with your hands until the inside is all mushy.

2

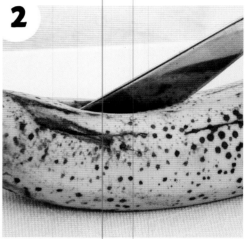

Use a dinner knife to cut holes carefully in the top and sides of the banana. This is how the butterflies will get to the mushy fruit.

3

Draw butterfly shapes onto pieces of paper in different colors. Carefully cut out the shapes.

4

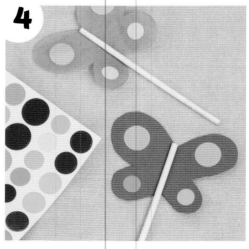

Stick circular stickers onto your shapes to make paper butterflies. Glue them onto lollipop sticks, then use them to decorate your banana.

A butterfly tastes through its feet! When it lands on the banana, it will taste it first, then use its long mouth to feed.

Butterfly spotter

Keep an eye out for different types of butterflies that might visit your feeder. How many can you spot?

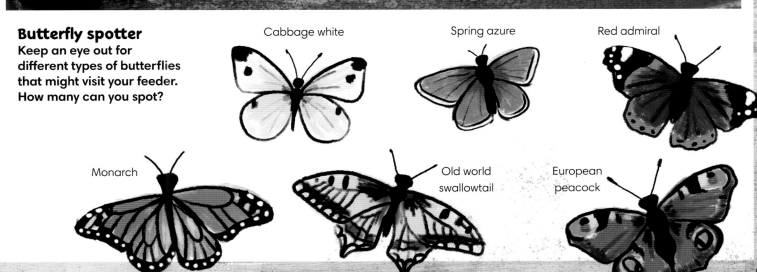

Cabbage white

Spring azure

Red admiral

Monarch

Old world swallowtail

European peacock

Pet's Corner

You can grow your own tasty treats for your pets. Cats, dogs, guinea pigs, and rabbits love to nibble plants, but it's important to provide them with ones they can safely eat.

You will need

- Plastic bottle
- Scissors
- Permanent marker
- Water bowl
- Gravel
- Compost
- Water
- Pet-friendly seeds

Grow in a sunny place and use well-drained soil. The seeds germinate within 1-2 weeks, and the grasses are ready to be nibbled after 4 weeks.

Sow barley, oats, and wheat for your rabbit. Sow Timothy meadow grass and plantains for your guinea pigs.

1

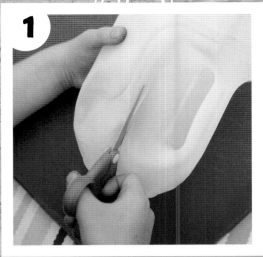

For the labels, cut a panel from a plastic bottle and then draw an outline of the shape of your pet with a marker.

2

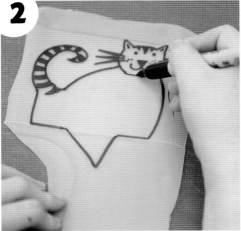

Add features, such as whiskers, using the marker. Then cut out around the pet shape.

3

Ask an adult to drill holes in the base of the bowl. Fill with a little gravel, then add compost. Water the soil.

4

If the seeds are large, such as cat grass for cats, cover them with soil, pressing down with your fingertips.

5

If the seeds are small, such as Lucerne grass for dogs, sprinkle them over the surface of the moist compost and add a thin layer of soil on top.

6

Keep the containers well watered as the plants grow. Trim the plants using scissors to keep them at a good height for your pet.

Recycled garden

Reusing and recycling in the garden is a great way to reduce your waste and live a greener life.

Why ReCycle in the garden?

Recycling is when you turn an old object or material into something new. You can sort your waste and send it to a recycling center. You can also reuse objects that are old or broken by finding new uses for them at home.

Why should I recycle?

Reduce pollution
Reusing objects instead of buying them new saves energy and the resources that it takes to make them. For example, making things from plastic consumes oil, which is a fossil fuel that takes millions of years to form underground.

As good as new
Plants and animals don't care if things are broken! Plants are just as happy to grow in cracked containers as in new ones.

Save habitats
Recycling and reusing helps the environment beyond your home and garden. Insects, birds, and mammals all need places to live and have their young. If we create more landfills to throw garbage into, more animal habitats will be destroyed.

How can I avoid waste in the garden?

Collect water to use on plants
A rain barrel catches runoff water from gutters and collects rainwater. This water can be used to water plants and fill ponds. Rainwater is better for plants and animals than tap water because it hasn't been treated with chemicals.

Don't buy it, recycle it
You can save money and the environment by reusing cans, bottles, pots, and tubs from around the home as containers. Just make sure there are holes in the bottom so water can drain out.

Composting
Food waste from the kitchen and grass clippings and leaves from the yard can be used to make compost. Not only does composting save green waste from being sent to landfills, but it's also a free way to add nutrients to the soil.

Recycle and renew

What can you do with all your fruit and vegetable peelings, old plants, grass clippings, and fall leaves? You can use them to make wonderful, rich soil or layers of mulch for the plants you'll grow next year.

Making your own compost

If you want to make compost but you only have a small space, you can buy a plastic compost bin. Add layers of waste that will rot down inside the bin and you'll have excellent, crumbly compost six to nine months later.

1 Choose a partly sunny site for the compost bin. Place the bin on ground and not concrete, so that water can drain out and helpful bugs can get in.

2 Keep filling your bin with equal amounts of "green" and "brown" waste to get the best mix.

3 Cover the bin with a lid, or an old doormat to keep in the heat to encourage the bugs. Sprinkle in some soil and, every month or so, ask an adult to help you mix the top few layers with a garden fork, so the waste will rot faster. You'll notice your heap rotting down and reducing in size. It will smell earthy!

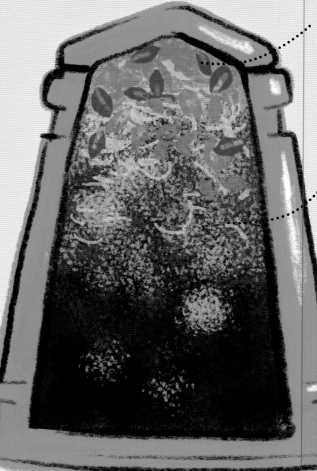

The **greens** are the young, wet waste, such as vegetable peelings, grass clippings, and tea bags, which will rot quickly. They provide nitrogen and moisture.

The **browns** are the tough, dry waste, such as paper, egg cartons, fallen leaves, and your pet's bedding. They provide fiber and carbon and form air pockets for the bugs.

Through composting, the goodness from decaying plants can be recycled and turned into rich soil for new plants to use.

Don't put these in your compost: cat litter, dog poop, disposable diapers, glossy magazines and newspapers, cooked food, oil, meat, or fish.

Compost critters

Rich, crumbly compost is partly made up of bugs' very dark poop. You'll see many busy bugs living in your compost bin. Some bugs feed on the green and brown organic waste you've put in. Others shred this waste and tunnel through it, mixing it up.

Smaller, organic-waste-eating bugs attract bigger bugs in search of food to the compost heap.

We all eat organic waste.

Millipede

Pill millipede

Garden snail

Slug

Compost mites

Earthworm

If you have these, you'll get these!

Look out! We eat smaller bugs.

Earwig

Rove beetle

Ant

Spider

Ground beetle

Centipede

The magic of mulching

Another great gardening tip is to try mulching. Mulch is a layer covering the surface of the soil that provides nutrients to the plants, keeps in the moisture, prevents weeds from growing, and helps to protect the roots from cold. Try tree bark, pine needles, grass clippings, and even seaweed. Recycled glass, beads, or seashells can be used as decorative mulch.

Make your own lovely leaf mold

Punch a few holes in the side and bottom of a trash can liner. Gather piles of fall leaves and put them in the bag. When the bag is almost full, sprinkle the leaves with water, then shake the bag and tie it up. Store it in a shady spot. After a year, the leaves will have rotted down into a rich, crumbly mixture. Spread this over your soil, and your plants will thrive.

Collecting seeds

Many of the plants you have grown have produced seeds that you can collect and then use to grow new plants next year.

You will need

Healthy plant

Scissors

Paper bag

The secret of success is to collect the seeds at the right time. Choose a dry, windless day to collect your seeds so they don't get damp or blow away.

1 Choose a healthy plant. When seed heads or seedpods have ripened, cut off the entire seed head or pod.

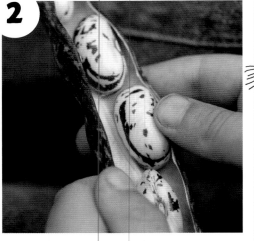

2 Remove the seeds using your fingers. Leave the seeds to dry in a warm place. Store the seeds in a dry, cool place until spring.

3 Some seeds that are very dry may need to be soaked before planting to encourage them to germinate.

4 Why not trade seeds with other gardeners and give some to your friends to plant, too?

Angelica seeds

Pepper seeds

Bean seeds

Sunflower seeds can be collected when they look big and brown. Pinch them out into a paper bag.

Eggshell Planters

If you've eaten eggs, you can put the leftover shells to good use by planting seeds in them. The shells protect your delicate seeds and even deter small creatures like slugs that would like to eat your seedlings.

1

Wash and dry leftover eggshells and put them back in the egg carton they came in.

2

Fill the eggshells with soil. Don't pack the soil too tightly. Sow one seed in each eggshell.

You will need

Clean eggshells

Egg carton

Quick-growing seeds, such as nasturtium

3

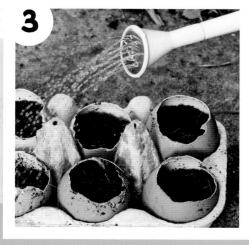

Water the eggshells and put them in a warm, sunny place. Either a windowsill or a bright corner of your yard would be good.

4

Give the plants a little water every day until the seedlings sprout. This should only take a week. If no seedlings sprout, move the carton to a warmer spot.

5

Once you have healthy seedlings, take them out of the carton and plant them in the soil. Eventually, you'll need to take them out of the eggshells so their roots can grow.

Crumble up eggshells and sprinkle them around your plants to provide nutrients.

Stunning Succulents

Succulents make gorgeous indoor plants, and they are easy to take care of. Once you have a succulent, you can create more of them by propagating them. This means growing a new plant from a part of the old one.

You will need

- Succulent plant
- Paper
- Tray
- Soil
- Spray bottle

1

Buy a healthy-looking succulent plant from the garden center. Pick one in a color you like, because you're growing more just like it!

2

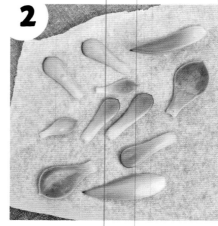

Gently twist and remove around 12 leaves—be careful not to tear them. Space them out on some paper, and let them dry for a few days.

3

Fill a tray with soil. Once the leaves look and feel dry, arrange them in a circular shape in the tray.

4

Spritz your circle with water, then keep spritzing it every day. After a week, you'll notice some tiny roots start to sprout from the ends of your leaves.

5

Eventually, tiny new succulents will start to sprout where the roots are. If you take care of them, they will grow into full-size succulents!

Grow a few
different-colored
succulents and create
a gorgeous rainbow
garden.

Cork Planters

You can find corks either stopping up bottles or being sold in craft stores. Using them to create mini planters is a great way to reuse them. Once you've grown some tiny succulents using the steps on pages 104-105, you can plant them in your corks.

You will need

Dinner knife

Corks

Craft glue

Magnet

Soil

Tiny succulent

Fridge

If your cork is too heavy and swings around on the magnetic surface, glue a second magnet above it.

1 Using an ordinary dinner knife, carefully scrape a hole in the top of a cork. Ask for help from an adult if you're not confident doing this.

2 Put a dab of craft glue on the back of a small magnet. Hold the magnet onto the side of the cork until the glue dries and the magnet sticks.

3 Fill the hole in the top of your cork with soil. Do not water, as water will make the cork soggy.

4 Plant a tiny succulent or other mini plant into the soil. Then make a few more cork planters!

Creative containers

Unusual pots for your plants will make your gardening projects extra interesting. Any container that has sides can be used, so keep a look out for possible ones to recycle, or make your own from a comic book or newspaper.

You will need

Newspaper
or comic book page

Water glass

Soil

Seeds

Keep your seedlings inside somewhere warm and bright during the winter months. Plant them outside in spring.

1

Take a page from a newspaper or comic book. Fold over one long edge, twice, to make the container.

2

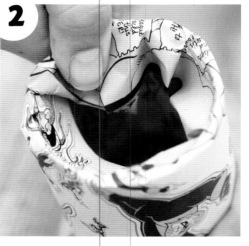

Roll the paper around a glass. Push the unfolded edge into the glass to make the base of your paper pot.

3.

Slide the paper off the glass. You can use the glass to help you flatten out the base of your pot against a table.

4

Fill the pot with soil and then it is ready for sowing the seeds. Once the weather is warm outside, the seedlings can be planted in their pots straight into the soil. The paper will disintegrate over time.

Almost anything can become a planter. Before you throw away an old or broken object, consider making it a home for a plant.

Pot labels and markers

When you plant seeds, remember to make a label. When seedlings appear, it may be hard to tell which plant is which. Your labels can be as simple as craft sticks with names written on them, or you can have some fun making and decorating more elaborate labels.

Tall labels

Labels on sticks will stand out in a pot. They are ideal for bushy plants, such as lamb's lettuce or herbs. Make waterproof labels using plastic pizza bases or the bottoms of plastic bottles.

Wildlife labels

Make a note of which plants are good at attracting wildlife—check the back of the seed packet for information. Waterproof labels can be made from leftover plastic.

Use a permanent marker to make the label waterproof.

Stone markers

Mark around where you've planted seeds with colorful stones. What eye-catching designs will you paint? Why not paint on some animals or the first letter of your name?

Paint me!

Funny markers

Plant funny ping-pong labels all over your garden. Simply make a hole in a ping-pong ball and stick it on top of a plant stake. Use waterproof pens and paint to decorate.

Craft-stick labels

Craft sticks are very handy as labels for small seed pots. Use pens to draw a picture of the vegetable you have planted or to make a pattern.

Paint the end of a craft stick to measure how deep to make your seed hole.

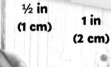

½ in (1 cm)

1 in (2 cm)

1½ in (3 cm)

basil

Mini greenhouses

Big greenhouses are used to grow fruit and vegetables that need warm temperatures to thrive. You can make mini versions for your windowsill to house some spiked cacti— they love a warm, dry place to grow.

You will need

Glass jar

Tape

Glass pen

Soil

Trowel

Paper

Cactus

Gravel

Water your cactus every two weeks between spring and fall. Do not water in the winter.

1

Place a piece of tape on a clean, dry jar. Using a special pen for drawing on glass, use the tape as a guide to draw patterns all over the jar.

2

When you're happy with your patterns, put some soil into the jar to create a habitat for your plant.

3

Carefully lower your cactus into the jar. Put a funnel made from paper around your cactus to stop soil from getting caught in its spines. Cover the roots with soil.

4

Remove the paper funnel. Cover the top of the soil with gravel. This looks good and helps the cactus grow. Now make more and create a greenhouse garden!

Strawberry boots

Did you know that you can grow delicious strawberries in your backyard? Planting them in a pot is fine, but it's much more fun to recycle old rain boots!

1

Ask an adult to cut a hole in the side of the boot. Make sure it's big enough to fit your plant's roots into.

2

Put a little gravel in the boots to allow for drainage. Add enough soil to come up to the hole in the side.

You will need

Rain boots

Scissors or craft knife

Gravel

Soil

Strawberry plants

3

Push a strawberry plant sideways into the hole, then fill the boot with more soil, almost to the top.

4

Place another plant into the top of the boot. Level off the soil and press down firmly. Repeat this with the other boot. Water both boots well.

5

Place your boots in a sunny spot and keep them well watered. The plants should make strawberries within 12 weeks.

Rub petroleum jelly over the sides of the boots to keep slugs and snails away.

Bird bathroom

Many gardeners put food out for birds, but few remember to give them water. A birdbath and shower will give them somewhere to drink and to wash, keeping them healthy and happy.

You will need

- Shallow bowl
- Clean pebbles
- Decorations
- Plastic bottle with cap
- Push pin
- Water
- String

Where to put it

Birds will only visit your birdbath if they feel safe from predators. Place the bath close to bushes, where they can fly to if they become alarmed. Don't put it next to ground-covering shrubs where cats could be hiding.

1

Cover the bottom of a shallow bowl with a layer of pebbles. Place the bowl on a small sturdy table or a level tree stump.

2

Add a small decoration such as a pebble sculpture, a flagpole, or a plastic frog to your birdbath.

3

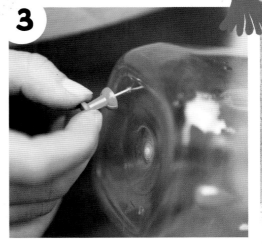

Make a tiny hole in the bottom of the bottle, using the tip of a push pin. Decorate the bottle if you like.

4

Add water to the bottle and screw on the bottle cap. The water will flow in a stream at first, then slow to a steady drip.

5

Attach the string to the bottle. Hang it above the bowl so that the water drips into it. The rippling effect will attract the birds.

6

Add some water to the bowl. Clean the bowl every few weeks with soapy water to remove droppings and bacteria.

Bird feeder

Watching birds in the yard is lots of fun, and they are easy to attract to your yard. All you need to do is hang up a feeder and fill it with the food that birds love to eat.

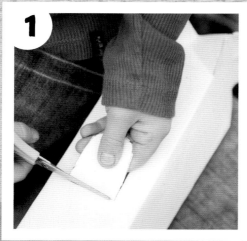

1

Cut a hole in the side of the clean carton about 2 in (5 cm) from the bottom to make a doorway. Ask an adult if you find this tricky.

2

Cut out brown and green leaf shapes from plastic bags and stick them on the carton with the glue.

You will need

Clean carton

Scissors

Plastic bags

Glue

Stapler

Wire

Twigs

Bird seed

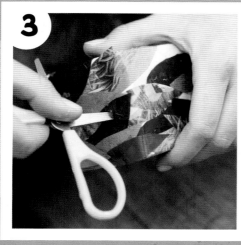

3

Poke several small holes in the bottom of the carton with scissors so that rainwater can drain out.

4

Staple the top closed. Pierce a hole in the top and thread the wire through to hang up the feeder.

5

Poke a twig through the carton just below the doorway for a perch. Add bird seed and hang the feeder.

There are about 10,000 different species of birds in the world.

House sparrows are the most widely spread wild bird around the world, but their numbers have declined dramatically in recent years.

House sparrow

Rufous-winged sparrow

Owl nesting boot

Owls mainly come out after dark. If you're lucky, you might spot one of these amazing birds. Give them somewhere to nest and listen for their distinctive hooting call.

You will need

- Adult-size rain boot
- Skewer
- Wood shavings or sawdust
- Wire
- Stepladder

1 Ask an adult to poke holes in the bottom of the boot with a skewer so that the rainwater can drain out.

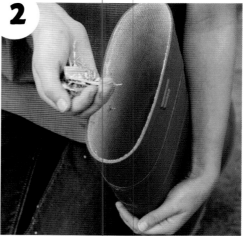

2 Drop two handfuls of wood shavings or sawdust into the boot as bedding for eggs and owlets (baby owls).

3 Secure the boot in place by wrapping wire around the branch and boot. Use a stepladder to reach a high branch.

4 Look for signs of use, such as white owl droppings. After the owls have left, clean out the boot and add more sawdust so it's ready for the next family of owls.

Many natural nesting sites are under threat. This treetop refuge will give small species of owl somewhere safe and warm to raise their young.

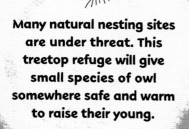

Bird experts think there are 217 different species of owl in the world, including snowy, tawny, and barn owls.

Self-watering Seedlings

Plastic bottles make excellent planters for growing seeds into seedlings. These clever planters allow the seedlings to drink as much water as they want. Turning bottles into planters is also a good way to reuse plastic so it doesn't end up in a garbage dump.

You will need

Plastic bottle

Pencil

Scissors

String

Water

Soil

1

Using a pencil, poke a hole into the soft plastic top of a clean water or soft drink bottle.

2

Cut the bottle into two parts. Cut about two-thirds of the way up the bottle so that the top part is shorter. The edges are sharp, so be sure to ask an adult to help.

3

Using the pencil, poke a length of string through the hole in the bottle top. This will allow the plant to drink.

4

Fill the bottom of the bottle with water. Put the top of the bottle into the bottom, with the cap facing down and the string dangling into the water.

5

Fill the top of the bottle with soil. Plant one or two seeds of your choice and put them in a sunny spot to grow. No need to water!

Poke a few holes in the cap of a plastic milk bottle and transform it into a watering can.

Glossary

Aphids
Tiny green insects that eat sap and can cause a lot of damage to plants. Ladybugs eat aphids.

Bud
A tiny part on a plant's twig or stem that grows into a leaf.

Bulb
A round, underground part of a plant that can be planted to grow into a full plant. Bulbs include onions and many spring flowers.

Cactus
A spiny plant that can store water inside its stem.

Carbon dioxide
A gas that plants need to create their own food through the process of photosynthesis.

Carnivorous plant
A plant that catches and eats insects.

Compost
A rich mixture of decayed plants that is added to the soil.

Crop
The harvest of fruits or vegetables that you get from a particular plant.

Eco-friendly
Any activity that minimizes the impact on the environment and helps, rather than harms, nature.

Ericaceous soil
Acidic soil suitable for growing plants such as blueberries.

Fertilizer
A mixture that encourages plants to grow.

Flower
The part of a plant where the male and female parts are found. Flowers usually have bright, colorful petals to attract insects.

Fruit
The part of a plant that forms when a flower is pollinated. The fleshy part protects the seeds inside.

Germination
When seeds sprout and start to grow.

Habitat
The place where an animal lives. Different animals prefer different types of habitat; for example, frogs enjoy ponds.

Hibernation
Sleeping through the winter months to save energy.

Hilling
Building up soil around a potato plant's stem to encourage it to send outroots where new potatoes will grow.

Marginal plants
Plants that can grow with their roots in the water at the edge of a pond.

Microscopic
Smaller than you can see with your eyes.

Mold
Another word for fungus. Some molds attack plants. Molds can grow quickly in waterlogged soil.

Mulch
A thick, protective covering on the surface of the soil that keeps in moisture, prevents weeds from growing, and helps to protect the roots from cold. Some mulches also add nutrients to the soil.

Nectar
A sweet liquid that flowers use to attract bees and butterflies.

Nutrients
Substances that help a plant or animal to grow.

Ovary
One of the female parts of a flower. Ovaries contain tiny ovules, which grow into seeds.

Oxygenation
Putting oxygen into water or the air.

Photosynthesis
The process by which plants make their food. It requires carbon dioxide gas and sunlight to take place.

Pest
Any bug or animal in the yard or garden that harms plants.

Pollen
Tiny grains that are carried from flower to flower by pollinators.

Pollination
The process where pollen is carried from one flower to another so that it can start seed growth.

Pollinator
Any insect or animal that carries pollen from one flower to another. Pollinators include bees and bats.

Pollution
Dirty and harmful substances that damage the environment.

Propagation
Growing new plants from parts of a plant, such as the leaves.

Pruning
Cutting back some parts of a plant to help the whole thing grow.

Recycling
Using materials again instead of throwing them away.

Ripening
When fruit grows to its full size and becomes ready to eat.

Root ball
The tangled mass of roots at the bottom of a tree.

Seed
A part of a flowering plant that contains a baby plant and a supply of food to get the seed started.

Seedling
A young plant that has just begun to grow.

Sprout
A spiny plant that can store water inside its stem.

Stake
Usually made of bamboo, stakes are stiff rods that can be used to support plants as they grow.

Stamen
The male part of a plant. It is where pollen is stored.

Stigma
One of the female parts of a plant. This is the part of the plant that recieves pollen from other flowers so the plant can make seeds.

Style
Connects the stigma to the ovary in a flower.

Succulent
A type of cactus that has fleshy leaves and comes in many colors.

Transplant
To move a young plant that has outgrown its pot into a larger container.

Vegetable
The edible leaf, stem, or root of a plant. Some plants that are called vegetables, for instance, bell peppers and tomatoes, are actually fruits.

Index

A

animal droppings 55
ants 56, 97
aphids 54, 56, 84
aquatic soil 9

B

bananas, overripe 88–89
barley 90
barn owls 121
beans 38–39
bee hotels 82–83
bees 7, 54, 57, 58, 60,
          80–83
beetles 57, 97, 114
beets 22–23
berries 59, 61, 70
birch trees 65
bird feeders 55, 118–119
birdbaths 116–117
birds 55, 56, 57, 58, 59,
          61, 70, 116–121
bird's foot trefoil 86
birds' nests 58, 120–121
birds of prey 57, 120–121
blueberries 46–47
borage 81
branched bur-weed 73
bugbane 87
bugs 56, 60, 61, 67, 68, 69,
          73, 74, 96, 97
bumble bees 83
butterflies 54, 57, 58, 60,
          86–89
butterfly feeder 88–89

C

cabbage white butterflies
          89
cactuses 110–111
carbon dioxide 9
carrots 18–19
cat grass 91
caterpillars 54, 56, 86

cats 91, 116
centipedes 60, 97
chickadees 54
chilies 30–31
chrysanthemums 69
clematis 64
common bladderwort 73
compost 8–9, 10, 95, 96
conservation 57, 94
container ponds 76–77
containers see pots and
          containers
cork planters 104–105
corn 42–43
craft stick labels 108, 109
creepy-crawlies 68
crocuses 69

D

daffodils 69
damselflies 114
decaying plants 96
deep water plants 72
dog roses 64
dormice 58
dragonflies 73
droppings 55, 117, 120
dwarf cattails 73

E

eco-friendly 4–5
eggplant 32–33
eggshell planters 100–101
eggs 7, 58, 86, 120
English lavender 81
environment 4, 5, 8,
          94, 95
European peacock
butterflies 89

F

fall 59, 69
ferns 69
fish 76, 77

floating plants 73, 77
flowers 6, 7, 54, 57, 62–63,
          80–81, 82
food web 56–57
fossil fuels 94
fossils 83
foxes 57
freesias 63
French lavender 65
French marigolds 87
frog homes 78–79
frogbit 73
frogs 57, 58, 60, 78–79,
          114
fruits and vegetables 4,
          14–15, 18–51, 55,
          59, 70, 96, 112–113
fuchsia 69

G

garlic mustard 86
glasses 106
glucose 9
golden club 72
grass clippings 96, 97
grass, long 65
green belts 57
greenhouses, mini
          110–111
grow bags 8
guinea pigs 90

H

habitats 56–57, 94
hair grass 72
health 5
heathers 80
hedges 60–61, 65
Helen's flower 87
herbs 16–17, 68
hibernation 58, 59, 60, 79,
          85
hollyhocks 81
homes 5
honey 58, 83

honey bees 83
honeysuckle 63, 81
hornwort 72
house sparrows 57, 119
hyssop 87

I

ice plant 87
indoor gardening 11, 102
insects 7, 54–65, 67–69,
          73, 74, 80–89,
          96–97, 114
ivy, common 65, 69

J

jars, glass 110–111
jasmine 63

K

kitchen garden 14–15

L

labels 108–109
ladybug sanctuaries
          84–85
ladybugs 54, 56, 84–85
larvae 114
lavender 63, 65, 69, 81
leaf mold 97
leaves 6, 7
leeks 26–27
lemons 50–51
lettuce 24–25
log piles 59

M

magnets 104
marginal plants 73, 77
markers 108–109
meadow cranesbill 81
mice 58, 60
michaelmas daisies 87
millipedes 97
mini hedges 61

mining bees 83
monarch butterflies 89
mosquitoes 54, 114
moths 57
mulch 9, 97

N

nasturtiums 86
native hedges 65
nature preserves, mini
    68–69
nectar 57, 62, 67, 80, 86,
    88
nests 70, 82, 120–121
nettles 86
newspaper 96, 106
newts 55, 58
nicotiana 63
night-scented plants 62
nutrients 6, 8, 10, 55, 56,
    95, 96, 97, 101
nuts 59, 61, 70
nymphs 114

O

oats 90
old world swallowtail
    butterflies 89
orchids 62
oregano 16–17
ovaries 7
owl nesting boot 120–121
oxygen 9
oxygenating plants 72, 77

P

pansies 69
parsley 16–17
peat-based compost 9
peppers 40–41
perfume 62–63
pest control 54
petals 7
petroleum jelly 113

pets, plants for 90–91
photosynthesis 9
plants 6–7
plants for wildlife 64–65
plastics 94
pollen 8, 43, 54, 62, 80
pollination 43, 54, 62, 82
pollution 94
pond dipping 114–115
pond skaters 114
ponds 72, 74–77, 95
potatoes 20–21
pots and containers 15,
    95, 106–107
predators 57, 116
propagation 102
pumpkins 36–37

R

rabbits 90
rain barrel 95
rain boots 112–113,
    120–121
rainwater 74, 75, 76, 77,
    95
raised beds 15
recycling 94–95, 96–97,
    106
red admiral butterflies 89
reeds 73
rodents 57
roots 6
roses 62, 64
rufous-winged sparrows
    119

S

sage, purple 80
scents 62–63
seasons 58–59, 69
seed collecting 98–99
seed potatoes 20–21
seeds 7, 8, 54, 55, 70,
    90–91, 100, 106,
    122–123
self-watering planters

122–123
slugs 57, 97, 100, 113
snails 56, 57, 60, 97, 113,
    114
snowy owls 121
soil 8, 55, 56
spawn 58
spiders 54, 58, 97
spinach 28–29
spring 58, 69
spring azure butterflies 89
squirrels 55, 59
stag beetles 57
stakes 15, 70
stamens 7
stems 6
stigma 7
stone markers 109
strawberries 48–49,
    112–113
strawberry boots 112–113
style 7
succulents 102–103, 104
summer 58, 69
sunflowers 66–67, 80, 99
sunlight 6, 9

T

tadpoles 114
tawny owls 121
thyme 16–17, 80
Timothy meadow grass 90
toad homes 78–79
toads 58, 60, 78–79, 114
tomatoes 44–45
tools 10–11
trees 15, 70–71

V

vegetable peelings 96
vegetables see fruits and
vegetables
verbena 81
voles 61

W

waste 5, 95, 96–97
water 9, 10, 69, 74, 95,
    122–123
water beetles 114
water bugs 74
water forget-me-nots 73
water hawthorn 72
water lettuce 73
water plants 72–73, 75, 77
watering cans 11, 123
wheat 90
wildflowers 64
wildlife 4, 54–91, 94,
    114–121
window boxes 68
windowsills 14, 110
winter 59, 69
worms 55, 56, 97

Z

zucchini 34–35

Acknowledgments

DK would like to thank: Clare Lloyd, Hélène Hilton, Becky Walsh, and Abigail Luscombe for editorial help; Helen Peters for the index.

The publisher would like to thank the following for their kind permission to reproduce their photographs:

Key: a=above; b=below/bottom; c=center; f=far; l=left, r=right, t=top.

1 Dreamstime.com: Bidouze Stéphane / Smithore (b).
4 123RF.com: Iryna Denysova (bl). Dreamstime.com: Marilyn Barbone (cr). 10 Alamy Stock Photo: AidanStock (br); Alexander Vinokurov (ca); Metta focus (cra); Metta foto (cl); Sergey Skleznev (cb); Kevin Wheal (bc). 12 Getty Images: Will Heap (tl). 16 Dreamstime.com: Stocksolutions (br). 18 Dreamstime.com: Stocksolutions (cl). 20 Dreamstime.com: Stocksolutions (cl). 22 Dreamstime.com: Stocksolutions (cl). 24 Dreamstime.com: Stocksolutions (cr). 26 Dreamstime.com: Slogger; Stocksolutions (br). 28 Dreamstime.com: Stocksolutions (cr). 29 123RF.com: Nataliia Melnychuk (b). 30 Dreamstime.com: Stocksolutions (cl). 32 123RF.com: Nataliia Melnychuk. Dreamstime.com: Stocksolutions (crb). 34 Dreamstime.com: Stocksolutions (cr). 36 Dreamstime.com: Stocksolutions (cl). 38 Dreamstime.com: Stocksolutions (cr). 40 Dreamstime.com: Stocksolutions (cr). 42 Dreamstime.com: Stocksolutions (cr). 43 123RF.com: Songsak Paname. 44 Dreamstime.com: Stocksolutions (cla). 46 Dreamstime.com: Stocksolutions (cl). 47 Dorling Kindersley: Alan Buckingham (tr). Dreamstime.com: Richard Gunion / Shootalot (tc). GAP Photos: (b). 48 Dreamstime.com: Stocksolutions (cr). 50 Dreamstime.com: Luis2007 (c/Background); Stocksolutions (cl). 51 123RF.com: Weerachai Khumfu (tl). Alamy Stock Photo: Martin Shields (b). Dreamstime.com: Christian Jung (tc); Lestertairpolling (tr). 52 123RF.com: Papan Saenkutrueang (bl). Dreamstime.com: Shih-hao Liao / Photoncatcher (cl). 53 123RF.com: Blend Images (bl). 54-55 Dreamstime.com: Adistock (Background). 54 Dreamstime.com: Thai Noipho (cr); Svetlana Larina / Blair_witch (clb, cb). 55 123RF.com: 5second (b); Timothy Holle (cl); Denis Tabler (c); Marie-Ann Daloia / mariedaloia (c/Squirrel); Eric Isselee (tr). Dreamstime.com: Shih-hao Liao / Photoncatcher (cr); Tomert (c/Photo frames). 57 Dreamstime.com: Stephen Griffith (tr). 58 Dreamstime.com: Artjazz (cr); Prentiss40 (cl). 59 Dorling Kindersley: Oxford Scientific Films (cr). Dreamstime.com: Volodymyr Kucherenko (cl). 60 Dorling Kindersley: Liberty's Owl, Raptor and Reptile Centre, Hampshire, UK (bc). 60-61 123RF.com: Jürgen Fälchle (c). 61 123RF.com: William Rodrigues Dos Santos (br). Dreamstime.com: Mikelane45 (bc); Susan Robinson / Suerob (bl). 62 123RF.com: Igor Terekhov (bc); udra (bl). Dreamstime.com: Whiskybottle (br). 63 123RF.com: annete (br). Dreamstime.com: Phanuwatn (bl); Alfio Scisetti (cla). 64 Dreamstime.com: Andrew Oxley (clb). 65 Depositphotos Inc: Arrxxx (cla). Dreamstime.com: Jochenschneider (tl); Mysikrysa (bl). iStockphoto.com: Martin

Wahlborg (clb). 66 Dreamstime.com: Stocksolutions (cla). 67 123RF.com: Robert D Hale (b). Dorling Kindersley: Peter Anderson / RHS Hampton Court Flower Show 2014 (tl). Dreamstime.com: Alfio Scisetti / Scisettialfio (tc). 68 Dreamstime.com: Stocksolutions (cl). 69 Dreamstime.com: Adistock (Background). 70 Dreamstime.com: Stocksolutions (cr). 71 Alamy Stock Photo: Avalon / Photoshot License. 72 123RF.com: PaylessImages (cb). Dreamstime.com: Kewuwu (ca); Verastuchelova (cla). 72-73 Dreamstime.com: trekandshoot (b). 73 123RF.com: maxaltamor (ca/Sparganium erectum). Alamy Stock Photo: Frank Hecker (cb); M & J Bloomfield (clb). Dreamstime.com: Argenlant (ca); Toni Genes (cla). 74 Dreamstime.com: Stocksolutions (br). 75 Dreamstime.com: Luis2007 (Background). 76 Dreamstime.com: Stocksolutions (cl). 78 Dreamstime.com: Stocksolutions (cr). 80 Dreamstime.com: John Pavel (c). 81 123RF.com: Thanongsak Onhatpho (clb). Dorling Kindersley: RHS Hampton Court Flower Show 2012 (fcla); Mark Winwood / RHS Wisley (tl). Dreamstime.com: Michael Smith (cl). 82 Dreamstime.com: Luis2007 (Background); Stocksolutions (cl). 83 Dorling Kindersley: Neil Fletcher (br). 84 Dreamstime.com: Stocksolutions (cla). 85 Dreamstime.com: Kellie Eldridge (br). 86 123RF.com: Simona Pavan (bl). Dreamstime.com: Tt (cl). 88 Dreamstime.com: Stocksolutions (cl). 90 Dreamstime.com: Stocksolutions (cl). 92 Dreamstime.com: Stocksolutions (cl). 94 123RF.com: Phanuwat Nandee (tr). 95 123RF.com: windsurfer62 (br). 98 Dreamstime.com: Stocksolutions (cla). 99 Dreamstime.com: Rrodrickbeiler (tc). 100 Dreamstime.com: Stocksolutions (cr). 102 Dreamstime.com: Stocksolutions (cla). 103 Dreamstime.com: Harrydo (b); Taniawild (tc). 104 Dreamstime.com: Stocksolutions (cl). 106 Dreamstime.com: Stocksolutions (cla). 108 Dreamstime.com: Adistock (Background). 108-109 Dreamstime.com: Bidouze Stéphane / Smithore (b). 109 Dreamstime.com: Adistock (Background). 110 Dreamstime.com: Stocksolutions (cl). 112 Dreamstime.com: Luis2007 (Background); Stocksolutions (cr). 113 Dorling Kindersley: Alan Buckingham (br). 114 Dreamstime.com: Stocksolutions (cr). 116 Dreamstime.com: Stocksolutions (cl). 118 Dreamstime.com: Stocksolutions (cr). 118-119 Dreamstime.com: Luis2007 (Background). 119 123RF.com: Callum Redgrave-Close (br). Dorling Kindersley: Alan Murphy (bc). Dreamstime.com: Paul Reeves / Paulreevesphotography (bl). 120 Dreamstime.com: Stocksolutions (cl). 121 Dreamstime.com: Assoonas (br); Ondřej Prosický (t, bl). 122 Dreamstime.com: Stocksolutions (br). 123 Dreamstime.com: Luis2007 (Background)

Cover images: Front: Dreamstime.com: Luis2007 c; Back: Dreamstime.com: Artjazz clb, Luis2007 c, Sahua bc; Spine: Dreamstime.com: Luis2007 c

All other images © Dorling Kindersley
For further information see: www.dkimages.com